The *Storm*

By Emma Benoit

To my loved ones.

Foreword

Hi! I'm Emma Benoit. I am twenty-five years old and have been writing on and off over the last year. Writing for me is a cathartic way to express myself. I am an Indigenous queer artist who was born and raised in Newfoundland of Mi'kmaq descent. I have built myself a home in New Brunswick on Wolastoqey land. I take pride in my heritage and the home I have built for myself over the last six years.

Over the last year, I've compiled a booklet of my poetry and short writings that have helped heal me on my journey of mental health and my path to sobriety. Some of the pieces are dark, reflecting dark moments of my life's chapters, while others are light, like how I was feeling while healing.

The purpose of my poetry is to show my pain, healing, and self-discovery. I'm hoping to share this as I have discovered that pain shared is pain lessened. This past year has been a difficult journey for me, and I hope to inspire folks that things do get better in life, and to also reach out and ask for help when needed to heal.

Wela'lin

Table of Contents

Seasons

Fall

The leaves are bright,

Alive,

Whispering along with the wind.

The babbling brook

Commands you to stop in

Your tracks and take in each

Moment in stride.

The trees are whistling in the wind,

Inviting you in...

Dare you enter?

Camping

Hot coffee fills the air,

The warmth is like a big hug.

Outside, the world is moving fast.

If you take a second to stop to listen,

You'll hear the stories of the wind,

The memories of the moving brook,

And you'll realize...

What's the rush?

Life's Seasons

What if this season never ends?

What if the thoughts never go away?

So what if I just let me

And my feelings fade away?

Like fall into winter,

Like the clouds of a sunset,

Slipping away into the darkness of the night.

Winter

Crisp winter winds
Fill the air.
Mother Earth is alive
Breathing deeply
Into my soul.
I am awakened
By her cold breath.
I am learning to be patient,
Like a bear in hibernation.

Snow

Snowflakes falling down,
Leaving a crisp layer of white
On top of all of the bad.
Snow is a sign of a fresh start,
A new beginning.
It reminds me of when I was a little girl,
Who found so much joy in playing in the snow.
I hope one day that I find that same joy.

Spring

Spring is a beautiful, fresh start to a new season
of life.

The song birds sing,

The leaves replenish,

The flowers blossom.

Some say that the new year begins in January,

In the dead of winter.

However, I believe that the year begins in spring.

Welcoming life with open arms,

Warm winds,

And blossoming beginnings.

Withering

The Storm

They say there's always a calm before a storm.

A quiet, peaceful period before a period of great

activity, argument, or difficulty.

But what if there is no calm?

What if it's all a storm?

Do I continue to play this charade?

But how do I differentiate between calm and

storm

Where the gales blow sideways,

I can't see where to take a step.

When all I feel is the storm burning up inside of

me.

Am I the storm?

Am I somewhere in between?

Did the Creator set this fire inside of me to do

good by others?

Am I the storm that will break through the

generational trauma?

Ocean

This too shall pass,
Like an ocean wave,
Rolling out to sea.
But what if it doesn't?
Or what if the waves,
Of despair roll together,
Into a tidal wave
Of depression?
Will I too, be sucked
under and drown?
Or will I save myself?
Before it's too late...
Only time will tell.

Nostalgia

I long for the smell of fresh-cut grass

On a cold winter's day.

I crave the sensation of screaming songs

In the backseat of my best friend's car.

I scream a shriek of grief,

For all of the what-ifs and could-haves.

A wistful smile of walking through the woods

with old friends.

Sometimes, I think the hardest part of growing

up

Is missing the nostalgic parts of life that seem so

far away.

That seems like a lifetime ago,

Yet are so close to my grasp.

Emotions

A rush of emotions comes flooding in.

Washing away everything in its path.

Leaving behind an array of destruction,

Like a tsunami.

If you are not prepared,

You will be left behind with nothing.

Or even worse, death.

Mental Health

Why is getting help for mental health so hard?

No wonder we keep losing such bright lights to
horrible illnesses.

Change is necessary, and the time is NOW!

I do not want to become another statistic.

I am screaming, crying, and pleading for help.

Why won't they listen?

What if it's already too late for me?

What if I always feel this way?

Addiction

They say addiction is a disease.

It runs through the blood of my family.

It runs through the blood of my body and soul.

The grip is strong.

I grapple with it each and every day.

But I am stronger.

Addiction is a long, hard battle.

But so is staying sober.

So I am choosing my path in this life.

I am paving the way for our future generations.

I am choosing to stay sober.

I will be the one to break this vicious cycle.

Sobriety

Sobriety is a hard choice to make,
But so is addiction.
You need to actively choose which lifestyle
You want to continue to pursue it.
Both are extremely hard.
It's hard on everyone in your life.
Even the people who are cheering
You on from the sidelines.
Choosing sobriety has been one of the
Best choices I have ever made for myself.
I am choosing me each and every day.
I am choosing to continue
To break the generational cycle.
I am a proud survivor of such a
Debilitating disease known as addiction.

Relapse

They say relapse is a state of suffering,
Deterioration after a period of time.
What they do not say about relapse,
Is how beautiful life can be,
When you come out on the other side of it clean.
Unfortunately, some never do.
Some never get to see the light at the end of the
tunnel.
Others get lucky enough to experience a state of
recovery.
They say recovery can be defined as a
Process of change through which
Individuals improve their health and wellness.
With addiction comes relapse.
With relapse, can come disappearance or even
death.
However, without relapse, sometimes the path to
Recovery becomes jaded.
And sometimes, a relapse is the exact thing an
addict needs
To wake up and realize
That recovery is the only choice.

Grief

They say with grief,

Time heals all wounds.

I believe that with grief,

Comes a long process of sadness, anger, and even

self-doubt.

Deep sadness,

Anger of the lives lost too soon,

Self-doubt on why things happen the way they

do.

I believe that with grief comes great pain.

A pain only known when experienced

At a gut-wrenching level.

A pain so deep, you sometimes cannot see

The light at the end of the tunnel.

A pain so severe that you never believe that time

heals all wounds.

I believe that it is crucial to begin your grieving

journey

When you are ready to.

I think that with time, the grief may become a
little easier
However, it never goes away.
Grief can sneak up on you in mysterious ways.
You could be listening to music,
And a song plays that reminds you of them.
You could be shopping at the grocery store,
And see their favourite snacks.
You could be going through the motions of life
And think, hey, I should call them.
And in those moments, hold them close to
yourself.
Speak to them as if they were still here.
Keep their memory alive forever.

Rebirth

Sun

I sit in silence

Basking in the sun

Letting it kiss my cheeks

While I reflect on life.

The wins

The loses

The lost loves

The new loves

And the in-between loves.

Life is funny like that.

Your body never forgets.

One day, it will tell your story

It's up to you to choose to hear it

Or to continue to hide in the darkness of despair.

Sea Glass

Here's to new beginnings.

Like sea glass,

We fall into

Shattered bits and pieces,

Stuck amongst the heavy rocks

Of life.

We tumble,

We hide,

But we also prosper.

Because, like sea glass,

Your story doesn't end here.

As this is the beginning

Of a new transformation.

Evergreens

Evergreens are so resilient.

They retain their leaves,

as it is more energy efficient

than regrowth.

They weather each and every storm,

Standing stronger and taller than ever,

Absorbing what life has to throw at them.

We have a lot to learn from evergreens,

They continue to thrive,

They continue to remain strong

And sturdy in their roots.

Even on the hardest of days,

They survive.

Amara

I will see you in every sunrise.

Every time that an eagle soars by,

In each and every rainbow,

Until I see you again.

On our next journey.

Where our paths cross again.

Healing

Healing

A transformation can be so hard.

New beginnings bring up old ghosts.

However, they allow us to set them free.

After rock bottom, there will always be a rebirth.

And that, my friend, will be oh so rewarding.

Our Gardens

The garden can teach us all so much about how
to be successful in this lifetime.
Our gardens are full of wisdom,
Empathy,
Resilience.
They teach us that to thrive,
We must first ground ourselves.
They teach us that to be happy,
We must rest.
That we must fuel ourselves with rich nutrients.
That first, we must feel the pain to be resilient
And continue to heal.
Our gardens teach us that to flourish,
We must first return to our roots.
They teach us that we are one.
Our gardens are life.
They are everything.
We are one.

New Beginnings

New beginnings can be bittersweet,

Like a cold glass of lemonade in the summer
heat.

New beginnings challenge every fibre of your
being.

They dig deep below and wreak havoc

On old routines and habits.

They rip you down,

Leaving raw flesh and bone,

But once they have weathered the storm,

Those new beginnings

Blossom into a beautiful, clear path with room to
grow.

Mosaic

When life shatters you into a million pieces,
It isn't about finding all of the same pieces
That were once whole.
It's about looking out for new pieces,
Creating a beautifully coloured
Mosaic in its place,
Leaving a piece of each touched soul
In its once broken place.

Progress

Progress can be so hard to notice.

It starts with small baby steps

Towards a bigger picture.

Sometimes progress is slow,

It may seem as if you're not moving at all.

It may feel as if you're stuck in a rut.

But the first step to noticing your progress

Is to give yourself credit for how much you've

gone through.

To acknowledge the balance of both the good

times and the bad.

Love

Sometimes I wonder if I love too deeply.

Then I remember how hard this world can be.

Without softness, there is no love.

Without rain, there is no growth.

Without the storm, you can't appreciate the sunshine.

And without it all, you can't blossom.

Fall deeply in love with yourself.

So much so that it doesn't pain you

When others try to destroy you.

Love yourself despite your scars,

That prove you've won the battles

Inside of you.

Love yourself so deeply, like you are your best friend.

Love so deeply that you know your own self better than anyone else.

Home

Grieving for a long list of possibilities

Of what could have been

Or what should have been

Will always be on my mind.

What if I wasn't the difficult child

What if my life was the one that was difficult?

The place I once called home,

Will never be my home again.

I grieve and long for that to be the case.

But to me, home is no longer a place.

It is my chosen family, it is my people,

It is who I love and who loves me back

unconditionally.

Twenty Five

It was never our job to figure life out by a certain
age.

I feel as if 25 is a pivotal point in time.

Where everyone thinks they have to have

Their whole life figured out.

But it was never our job

To have everything figured out

It's our job to enjoy the small things.

Like waiting for your loved one

To walk through the door after work.

Or the smell of a fresh cup of coffee early

In the morning on your way to work.

A call from an old friend.

The small things really add up to the big things in
life.

When you look back in time

And realize that those little moments

Paint a big picture of the beautiful little life

That you have built for yourself.

Thank you for the support from my loved ones, both family and friends, for their contributions to making this book happen. Your support means the world to me. I could not have made this journey of mine a possibility without your love, support, and guidance during this new chapter of my life.

The purpose of sharing this is that I have come to discover that pain shared is pain lessened. This past year has been a difficult journey for me, and I hope to inspire folks to understand that things do get better in life and to also reach out and ask for help.

Thank you to everyone who has bought a copy of my book. It means the world to me to be able to share a small part of my life's journey with you all. I hope you enjoyed sharing my pain, heartache, healing, and self-discovery throughout the reading of my poetry.

National Suicide Hotline Canada - 9-8-8

Kids Help Phone Canada - 1(800)668-6868

Emma Benoit
May 2025